Sympathy from the Devil

Kyle McCord

GOLD Wake Press

Boston, MA

Sympathy from the Devil

for my parents

Poems

One

Two

Three

One

I Write You This on a Train Named for an Endangered Bird

There are ways a story can't begin. Like pitting your protagonist
against an all-knowing, all-seeing jaguar spirit.
Or, worse, against an abstraction—like immorality or human unhappiness.
It could be argued that Hamlet's vengeance was doomed from the outset
because you can't fight for the dead, only against the living
who have enough problems as it is. Your Canadian brother-in-law
unemployed, rubs his knuckles while he sleeps.
A whole range of unadorable animals are on the docket for extinction.
I've identified some plot problems here. Like on New Year's
when Jeremy A's sister blew you in the bathroom
and midway through they threw you out of the house
without your high-tops: was no way to begin a story, and it did.
And I refuse to put bread on anyone's tongue and pretend it's flesh
to put cigarettes and fruit on a grave and pretend I intended it
more than an hour before. Why should it mean less?
The Confederate dead who haunt your city. Jeremy A's sister
years later aboard the California Zephyr. The blood rushing
to your extremities, the makeshift fan, the Mahler left open.
Even now, you can't play it perfectly—notes too far, too fast.
What do you want from any of us, reader? Elegy? Epiphany?
I am hunted by an all-knowing spirit who grows a shade over my head one day
and withers it the next.

Welcome to Unemployment, Massachusetts

It's a modest limbo we inhabit: corn tacos on Tuesday, enough anytime minutes
and uninvolved evenings. The aimless souls besiege your house
demanding to pick weeds from your garden for change.
Your mother allows it, while a woman you love is weeping
because the orchestras of the world sound worse for lack of funding.
The meals on credit and time, indeed, worse for being borrowed.
Eliot's Prufrock invites us to accept our role as the prom kings and queens
we were not. But, honestly, he was a sad, hard genius as so many of his era.
He didn't clip coupons or die face down in the Black Forest as others did
but in a show of humanity nearly lost his mind when his wife capitulated to
insanity. In this hive of inactivity, I drive through the darkened suburbs of Boston
where curtains thinly divide Monday from Tuesday, October from sailing season.
A fold of blurred strip malls. Says my Hebrew textbook: now you know the truth
even heaven is only two waters. There are three things Satan would do anything
to take from you. Instruct me what they are.

To Sarah Lost in a Latin American Love Triangle

You nurse wounds you don't even know you have.
You pen yourself into a poem where Hieronymus Bosch lines your nightstand
with intricate demonic goats and nymphs, and despite what you imagine
no one is better for it. Where the stars explode into stillness
and our friend cries to me about how you claimed she was drunk
and forgot her in a field a few miles north. How you were already leaving
Lorenzo's studio by the time she'd hiked back, bramble-bitten and tipsy.

A few crosswalks away, the aimless dead of one a.m. circle the gas station.
My eyes flutter at an astronomical rate, my muscles soften.
There's a moment where the irrevocability of a thing becomes evident.
The bone which was broken cannot be set. Like weeks earlier—
the shock of the coyotes stumbling upon us in the woods.
Those indistinct and trembling animals who we interrupted
but could not give back their moment of serenity.
The gas station slowed to an empty, illuminated lot.
You wrote, *I have bones I know nothing about. Every day I splinter
in a hundred different ways.* But it's not just what won't heal
worse, what about each of us seems so unwittingly ruinous:
the accidental intrusion, the coyotes huddled in the dark.

Ginny in the Dutch Master's Grove

Fourteen miles through storm-shattered forest
you knotted your hair to your head like an uncharacteristically slight Eve.
Did you know that the best translation of Adam is *earthling*?
The razor beaks of the birds you sketched shredded afternoon,
cawing while I examined how roots clawed
from their birthplace to the unlucky world above—
light which balds and the animals lapping their architecture.
Like in the paintings of the Netherlands, it seems best to stick to the main drags
the roads ragged where swaths of dense acrylic nip at the frame.

Greetings, earthling. I'm sure you tire of my constant questions, but I danced
on my heart after you shot me that one small smile by the horses
which seemed to wobble from the heat. Later, I primed one wall in the house
and all of a sudden, I saw the world as a series of frames
anxiously awaiting pigment, light, aroma. You talked about your father,
his unfed expectation, his Princeton education, and I thought
how Bruegel can capture us in a space so black, not even goodness can find us.
We want belief to fill us till we fall out of ourselves.
It's one of the hundred wrong reasons we marry.
When we close our eyes, sometimes a voice spins us about.
It seems everything in this forest is a small, paper ribbon of some sort.

Lycanthropy and You

I'm unprepared to push you through muscle and digit, inkwell
and out among the general populace of words. In Hebrew,
to write is easily confused with *to sever,* but then *to seize*
sounds like a werewolf; so I trust only these nerve endings ignited
because language means what it can't possibly.
Your caress rings even in the Quikstop where everything is built to spill
into the eye with a reckless animation: chips from the Spanish city of gold,
a man-sized, monocled peanut. It's important to get this right.
Quick, list all the synonyms you know for *abandon* and then all you know
of loyalty. We don't stand a chance in our own vocabulary.
The possums covered in young could be mistaken for a metaphor,
for strands of flax in the lamplight of suburban Des Moines
where you to attempt to ignite the moon with a clove over an unfinished
squabble from a previous existence. You were two fugitives on the run
from a common fate, much as you and I are now. And I'm not ready to sever
by mute calculation you from the lunar landscape (from me)
via loaded pen—whatever we are smeared across a page.
Let the werewolves seize this city. Let the record show
there is no record. That all is bleak beside the body, beside where the sky
climaxes into twilight behind me. Beside the wind chimes happening
into each other, it is the dead of winter.

The Ferry Took Me to the Mountain Pass

The ferry took me to the mountain pass that led to betrayal. Thin, penitent
snow orbed last October's crops where you were—hundreds of miles away
and going by the name of a long-forgotten Big Band star.

You called to tell me how your mother defected to another man and missed
her return flight from Honduras, never rescheduled. And the airline
left heartrending messages for your father through Christmas.

There are convictions deeper than loyalty which can tear you down to a husk,
you said. A houseplant harboring sunlight, a living room paralyzed into mold
and dust. In a room with a girl called Velvet, I lay listening to your breathing

like the car pushing snow-blind through the drifts. The girl's breath filling
my diaphragm, her curls bubbled over her breasts. Some people say
Abraham sacrificed Issac up on Mount Mariah, but I don't know that I believe it.

Eventually, the snow stops. The ship circles back. A searchlight
forms elegiac mirrors on the water. The mirrors are full
of the abandoning monsters we could never leave.

Poem for Lars von Trier from the Heart of Missouri

The Romantics might laud the importance of the poet returning to nature
but what about when fawns eat the pages out of my notebook?
My work is full of bored, aggravated bees.
At times, I'm tempted to trade in our hybrid for a hatchback
and dump meth by-products into the open stream.
Someday, we'll have the lab of our dreams
but for now this flophouse will have to do. This loincloth
and weasel pelt will have to work until our hours pick up. Until Pottery Barn
begins hiring again, this garden snake will be your garter belt.
Earlier today, I bought a Creedence album for a dollar eighty-one and regret it.
I'm sorry. I don't mean to yell. I don't mean to chase deer out of our dreams.
The easiest way to understand nature's brutality is through the eyes of a
misogynist. He hallucinates love for his wife. Tiny acorns accost his gutters
and collect in his deck slats. My inability to empathize isn't all that interesting.
It's your civility that saves us, says don't go to bed angry.
It's our third strike at this Denny's, and let's just do what the man says.
And after you calmly close the car door, I can let go what hardships
nature imposes. The titration tank rattling in the back, your hand,
a speckled loon asleep. The sky above Branson's the second coming,
unwitting suicide bombers explode.

Like the Fox Scheming for Eggs

Today, I swear you said, "Such a pretty God," lifting a soil sample
where late afternoon blended to a gossamer light on high-rises.
Step by step, you're becoming the kind of garbage collector
the world needs. For example, when you tore off your name tag
and sewed "International Sufferer" in its place
your laughter closed up a young man's war wound.
A vengeful spirit abandoned the body it inhabited. A thick fog
boggled the truck. I flick a cigarette, and sometimes what we call the sublime
is only an ancient John Denver eight-track played on repeat.
Sometimes my pen resembles a lamppost blurred by snow.
What are you writing? you ask. How do you spell *candelabra*?
Depends what you mean, you reply. I wonder if the rapture might be heralded
by an act as simple as that: an exchange, the slamming of a car door,
a motion detector blinked to life from a kiss on the cheek,
the garbage disposal waking the dog. A war starts over a botched parade
and takes the meat off my calf. When I feel pain there,
the doctors call it phantom pain, and I think of fireworks.
In 1852, game birds overran a mining town in Idaho but left more eggs
than the populace could eat. The moral seems too obvious. Evil doubtlessly
tampers with our destinies, you say. I nod, my hand on my wire on my chest.
I'm silently building my case against you. You're just the sort of do-gooder
I've traveled through time to stop.

Dolphins, the Scientists are Discussing Your Enormous Brains

They break out champagne in the breakroom, in the lab, in the streets
they are talking you up at all the parties.

But, I've never seen you
in the library after hours when I am shuffling through the awful cement maze,

never witnessed a dolphin tending the wounded at an accident.
Bring me the one you call Dr. Dolphin.

Outside my childhood home was a decrepit barn
where the floor rotted in and all our rain corralled there.

In the grotto, you could see yourself, the barn
all upside down, broken in.

This is my world to you—
vandalized, nails jutting one odd direction or another?

A child points to the horizon where one of your kind clears a fiery ring.
Johnny Cash plays his best despite being entombed in a small town in Tennessee.

At the great conferences of the world, the scientists have forgotten themselves
in furious debate over your frontal cortex.

They worry you will come to worship data as we do
while your beak's stuck in some plastic bottling.

Meaning, in the heat of love, we may forget to love.
There are reasons to fear what is tender.

Poem Without Manners

Dear Nancy Drew, did you catch me earlier, gawking as you dredged
the bog for an ancient scepter? I slammed the book shut before I could see.
One could lose their grip riding trains in the Outback. An aged pensioner
nudges me awake and makes some declaration about Gallipoli. A splotchy cosmos
printed on the seats reminds us we are akin to astronauts, drinking in recycled air
then artificial night. It hits each of us like a mysterious gas. How do you feel
about the German love affair with railways? Without the werewolf seductress,
there is no "Europa," no "Wolfenstein" without its pixilated, fascist inhabitants.
If no Beatrice then how will I ever escape hell? I face the fear
that I might wander these continents long after your hint of almond perfume
fades from the page, after salt thrown over a shoulder
over a curse has settled.

Nancy, can I call you Tracy? Sweetheart? I was born an old Satchmo of a soul
and how long do you think we actually have to feel happy?
One could lose their sense of scope seeing so much of their twenties
through protective glass. Ewes trot unsteadily along the meadow which washes
by like a plate. Late August coming on with its tuft tail and varicose leaves
shedding toward minimalism above where a sweet but slow-witted girl is walking.
She glances up from a poem where her life is over. Tracy, I want that
to be something you can solve: the mystery of the covetous father.
A city is hopelessly lodged in the girl's eye, and every branch
which does not bear fruit surely burns, her father tells her and returns to his paper.
Every branch which burns also longed to blossom, she thinks.

Some Admonitions to the Architect of Lust

If you are asked to choose guns or knives, choose guns and knives.
The townsfolk have it in for you. The militant Arabs also.
The animals who mate for life dream of your blood and Batman.
He puts up his batsignal out of boredom and hopes a hot meal awaits him.
I'm guessing you're the kind of girl who bicycles all over town.
I feed stray animals with love alone, which constitutes animal cruelty.
By day I am an efficient pound owner, but by night my spirit slinks
across the floor. I lay my head on the counter, and Satan appears
in the foyer. He follows my eyes, offers me meaningless trinkets.
He is bored as Batman. We both are. We agree we want the world
to cave in around us if only to feel something certain inside.
To look inward and see something steeled and shattered
and admit: you already half-way wanted it.

Childhood with Hypnopompic Overture

Our shared fear, friend, is that we were children abandoned on a boat
with one oar. You've rowed tirelessly on since before the invention of memory
but when I count backwards from ten, you will begin to pack away in an attic
the listless stares of those thick adolescents in stained camo overcoats
who couldn't conceive how you'd arrived here. Their eyes
like ruptured stars, sucking in everything in a wordless vacuum.
Nine, in a mythical brick fort with the radiators too close for code, and, eight,
how many second-degree burns did you see? Seven, and hunter's education's
a required course no matter how much your father protests.
But this, six, slips out your ear onto the floor like army ants
in a cartoon. You reach into your pocket for a flask from which, five, you dump
that afternoon when Jared, who'd repeated tenth grade three times, pushed
the effeminate boy down some steps, cracked his ribs with steel-toed boots.
Four, and you'd have forgotten it all, painting miniatures in sanguine and cyan
in your parents' basement, three, if everything in the town weren't so tiny.
Miniature bakery, pocket-sized barbershop, and as you row on
into memory, the water swishes away their tiny prejudices and slights
that couldn't help but become part of you, two, the way a landslide makes
shattered pillars and splintered doors features of a home. One, as it flows
with demonic speed from the hills with the snap of a finger: a weary
muscle which wakes you under clouds and the smell of dusted wood, a dock
wriggling beneath your back.

Poem for Rude Birds

Sometimes a siege is lifted when a mad dog assassin scalds off his own hand
in the presence of a king. Sometimes, you say, crazed disregard for the self
is all we have. For weeks you'd flogged yourself over a failed marriage
while the American auto industry burned down Detroit until only miles
of chained-up factory remained. And your regrets had been expecting you
elsewhere, in New York. Walking for years between twelfth
and twenty-third, schlepping boxes of old records, plates at the diner,
while rude birds pelted you with cryptic commands. I said look at your wrists
Nina, and you moved your hand below the tablecloth in embarrassment.
Everyone takes you too seriously you say and title one painting this.
When it's written all over your face how long you've been with anyone
you title another. In one acrylic, a family is lost in the land beyond goodbye.
The wharf attendant unties the ferry, and it slogs through the harbor.
You don't know it yet, but you're there too, waving to the handful of lovers
you've actually known but who can't make you out from the bow of the ferry.
Stop waving, I plead, but maybe you glimpse something I haven't—
maybe more than one lover is weeping and begging to return. Maybe the marble
sea cracks, the campfires of thousands of others rattling shadows onto the hillside.
Today is the day you will blend those birds into the background.

This is just to say I left the bottle of pinot beside the bathtub. I needed
to envision you doing something painstakingly illogical—the wine
turning your hair into an afterlife of a vine,
filling your shower with ink. It looked like my brother's hair
felt after chemo, and I thought about the consistency of acid rain.
This evening, I am having trouble writing coherent letters to the dead.
You cook up a joke involving ingestion of noxious chemicals
and I say I'll take it. Geese form a wreath and hover, and we entitle it
You can't imagine how little can hold us back. Sometimes I want to stay up
sawing you in half just to feel the snap of your sternum perfectly reset,
hip bones aligned, and you approach me like night's horse trotting up the cobbles.
I meet each night as a surly Tom Sawyer. I intrude in your dreams
without intending it. At night, you fall asleep in our poverty
and see your breath in the air conditioner.
You wake up hungry for plums.

They Said You Were to be a Conquistador

Dear Sarah, I'm writing to admit to you I've never made much of a Viking.
But you, your last name even sounds like stabbing. Your arm thrust in the air
drives the hibiscus to form a violet cloud out by the lighthouse.
Greetings from cattle-country Australia and moo.
I'm writing to tell you your figure is much too fine for insurance.
I could see you in some heavy chainmail. I could see you eating off a spit.
In Australia, an artist built an exhibit out of mirrors and ladders where he claimed
you could climb from heaven to hell. No one tried it. He lives on a beach now.
Maybe it is just like that. We're trapped in an era where simplicity may be
ingenuity, where what tempts me isn't all that elaborate. Sometimes, Sarah
a train passes so close to my body I can taste the silence
and I think my effort to describe it's both heroic and orthodox. I never
imagined how hard it would be here in the land of elephantine plants.
The shadow of my family line falls over me, or is it a line of latitude?
I pray past the hills mottled with flowers, the combusted silo,
past the ships silver with fish, the sky offering up a rib.

On String Theory and Other Problems of the Heart

Because it is possible for a black hole to tear open the middle of this arcade
or for our universe to be a lyre with infinite strings
which change their tune as you snap a satin bow into your bangs,

I am having trouble affixing on just one thing. Your mouth
or more importantly what you were saying about transporting
arsenic from Columbia. I lived through an era

when you could still see your loved ones to the door
to the causeway that exited into the Twin Cities or Detroit.
Vegas now. My spirit guide says your name

isn't important, but I know it means *constant*.
After our grand tour of your studio, I stopped writing
about the Franciscans. Dreamt of the sun cut by blinds

where I was how many impulses from your belt?
From what never would have worked?
What's intellect worth if it kills a part of you

that would carry dangerous chemicals across borders for love?
God's love is infinitely dense and dangerous and vanishes
into our body as bread. But I never asked to eat God.

I asked to occupy one of the sixteen cobalt earths you burned
into being in your lab coat one unbearably hot night in North America.
Outside, the nebula of buckshot. The lovesick jutting out their thorns.

According to quantum mechanics, most of everything happens
in a realm so subtle it might not be happening. Like the bobsled
factory where I imagine we work. Where I am carrying my lunch pail,
you are lacquering a ski. I wave. You wave at my wave
and pretty soon we've all put aside any notion our physical
experience is irreconcilable. You inspect all the bobsleds
atop an aging mechanical bull. The girls giggle whenever you go by.
I've asked them a number of times not to, but my irises turn to herons
and my hands don't fit folded to my chest. The girls can't stifle a laugh
when my hands wind up somewhere utterly inexplicable. Like when they made
the news in Southern Arkansas describing what the tornado sounded like—
As if the devil himself pulled the drain out of the air. Or when they were released
from prolonged captivity in Tehran. What can I do with such hands?
What would Mary Ruefle do in such circumstances? Delete. Delete.
According to quantum mechanics, no one can let the cat out of the bag
without breaking a commandment. This is another conundrum
that burdens me as I stare out on the finishing floor. A professor once asked
a classmate, *What makes you so afraid of dying alone?* Two trains are passing
each other on a platform. The man on one train has set his watch exactly
to the watch of a woman on the other train. Are these paid professionals
or just lonely individuals? I ask. According to my professor, it does not matter.
We are all just hobbled, he says, *quietly attempting to rise.*

Two

Sometimes I am a dog who has been shot into space via cannon.
In the space station, I race back and forth in front of the observation portal
where the crane gathers useful soil samples. What do I care for what is useful?
Who of you will throw the frisbee? Please, will some human hand
stroke my overcoat and inform me my relief will arrive shortly?
But nothing can save me from the David Bowie album I'm becoming,
drumming my paws to the sound of my own devolution. My master
has taken another, and I hear the animal's woofs and flops when he reassures
me via video monitor. Who will even bother with this confession?
Frisbee, art thou a frisbee of the mind, a false creation
as the rubber newspaper with which the master once baited me?
The probes return with their sleep-colored soil samples. I dream I am a man
living an odd but ordinary existence. I lie in the observatory and wonder
what primitive memory has made me dream of such desires, of solemn Pella
that hamlet of overgrown roses and the rapping of lovers in October.
The probes enter and set about clanging iron pots. Today, the second to last
good man on earth has died. You are now the only one left, and you have no
intent to die like this: dressed as a matador, your hand clutching your boss' wife's
thigh.

To Me at Twenty-Six, Star-Crossed in Sydney

Twenty-six years and my skin hasn't given up on the sensation
of intense solar radiation. In Arizona, heat valences fell like petals
while they drove my mother to the hospital with her husband, an expert
and enemy of executions by the state. I've not thought much
about the inhuman flame generated by the flow of electricity
into the nerves of a convict since I was eighteen. Billy Bob Thorton
put it in perspective—"Monster's Ball" on the bed with Sarah whose hair
was an immaculate raven diving for flecks of bread. A belief that hate can make
you something else—my father always understood that and so stayed away
from the fray even over something so insidious, he says when I'm twenty-two
and he returns to cooking. Blood red pepper, seeds and all, water chestnuts,
apricots. Dear Sarah, presently I'm in Australia. The Aboriginals,
many are in the ground with the earthquakes which are waiting for the right
moment to cut loose. All most of us has is what we ask for—today, a kebab,
some dates, the eucalyptus tree letting off an ellipse of shade. The shade swallows
up magpie chicks, their cream feathers still a gosling grey.
The native tribes gather their tired sorries from the state
who buried their forefathers in the Outback's heat. For my birthday
I'd like less warmth than the stars who have no pity. More than this black bag
yanked over half the earth. Less than the furnace that is mid-day in Darwin.
Only your arm on my arm—the dynamo of your breath catching in mine.

For Me at Twenty-Six, Impoverished in Sydney

In the morning, we move like vessels in a slothy fog
and want only what accommodates: the gum tree lowing
to my window, the elevator button blushing to life.
In your travelogue, you categorize my genus, species.
When in love, you say you know it by the torrents of spiders threshing your arm.
When October comes, you know it by the faces animated into vegetables.
Now it's August, and Aeneas clutches his lance
at the bow of his bronze ship. I walk into a miracle—the only planet
for parsecs where I can ford into the clairvoyant blue of waves.
Tonight, your Brazilian dances night into its coffin. Italy unfastens its bra
and looks back. Tide pools glow and I think of the beginnings of life
on Titan. Tiny methane-fed beings boogying in an underground river,
the river carrying the unintentional chimera of organic life—
something it can't even articulate, but scrawls its likeness on the rock face.
In August, Galvin's lovers write each other's names on the salt flats.
They slam doors. They throw their names into the wind like lances.
I come bearing daffodils, the many faces of Narcissus latched in a jar.

Useful Speculation

Say I am trapped in an elevator for a little over eight months, or say we meet up
in the past where we are both there to assassinate a little-known German baron
but can't agree ideologically. Say we squabble. Say personal problems
are at the root of most major religious conflicts of the twentieth century.
Says Luther, I don't care much for saints and exits stage right. Say God's politics
are that he flips ahead a few channels when the televangelist blinks on, droning
like the security announcements at the airport. Say even Satan covers his eyes
when rebels or governments are cutting off boys' hands
and throwing them in a bin. Say my calves itch from the cold and maybe hell
is a real place where people you meet, say at social functions, go
for a certain time frame. Say six to ten.
Say I make one silly hat for me and another for Sparkles
and then we all partake of a stiff drink out on the veranda.
Say you ask, "How did you manage for eight months?"
and I tell you how I could hear the echoes of others, and we would rap out
Christmas carols or show tunes to keep each other sane. Say someone
could go that deep into the vortex and return intact enough to raise a family.
Say in the debate over the Shroud of Turin, an Orthodox priest slips
and touches Jesus' face—is he smitten? Or smote?
You can't imagine God's exhaustion. Say we are around six feet tall
and move bipedally and can't work this out amongst ourselves.
Say Gabriel lowers his hands to his side and empathizes. Say he breathes out ash
and can't remember names. Say someone could venture so shallowly into a life
he says. Say this night rolling your bag along the streets of Melbourne
you fall in love. Say each of the trolleys and the statues of dead prime ministers
and the language formed by the drunkard punching out the bar window
shimmers. And even this is not meaning enough for your life.
You grow so selfish here in this city of owls.

Frankly, this scene just isn't working for me. So, an angel, an angel,
appears to our hero? The same guy who plays twenty matches
of chess at once and loses them all. The same guy who injures
his neighbor in an easily preventable gardening accident.
And is there an explainer in here as to why...no, you're saying no.
So maybe we work in some sort of divine roulette. Either way,
the angel offers our protagonist a chance to be a prophet, writer of revered
texts, and ravens are going to fly from his mouth with the regularity
of 747's out of SFO. Is that it? Or he can remain with Rebecca who,
don't look over at her now, is definitely mouthing something to me.
It's too aromatic in here, I think. I agree. Put Steve on that.
Steve? Ok, but our hero can remain with Rebecca who loves him
even though his apartment's some Bohemian rat hole and reeks
of tuna innards and he stands out on his patio with the green light
of some distant opulence hanging over him like an ideology. Do I have this?
I thought this was a story about a boy and his dog. Wait.
She's mouthing something again. All our sanctity is bunk
I believe. Put someone on that, please. Steve? Frankly
this whole flight from God shtick feels a little Jonah and Jonah
feels a little Gilgamesh. And when the hero says the ribbon of intrigue
pulls tighter around him each second, what does that even mean?
What does he mean I'm tired? If I've learned anything in this business
it's that every story is about a boy and his dog or his sled
or it's just space ape schlock. We need a boy with a sled
not some winged Jezebel. Steve, how fast
can you get that angel post-production presentable? The studio's
foaming up my nape already. Steve, what's with all this sanctity?
What does the script mean when it says sometimes there is nothing
which does not wish to be born? When the hero says I could barely
draw breath without you and plummets into the primordial sea. It says that here.
Cue the primordial sea beasts. What does that even mean?
I get it—the many atmospheres—it's the heart of God breaking
again and again. Clever. Steve, what's going on with the sanctity front? You, you,

get me some sleds. I want boys, I want dogs, one hour. I want to feel God's heart break, Rebecca. Someone cue waves. Someone, roll radiant, amber sea.

Faithful Poem to the Unfaithful Stars

After the month of mysterious rain, which made everyone wary
        and text each other endlessly.

After the bulls barreled through my poems and broke your electric
        toothbrush, your homespun dress brushed the driveway.

After you'd cheated on me, then with me on the guy after me, then
        with some other guy altogether,

but before the sparrow puffed up then seemed
        to famish into origami and it was October 20th. After bed bugs

ate our neighbors and haunted all our shopping excursions, a dawn
        of rumpled t-shirts split the blinds, after *Why didn't you tell me?*

and *I'm sorry.* After I slipped a pill, I slipped a pill before the facts were known
        and on the news, a German billionaire paid some dude one million dollars

to kill and cannibalize him. After what to the outside world
        made sense to exactly no one, except the remaining cannibal lover

and anyone studious of the lengths a person would pursue to feel true dedication.
        After Zodiac. After the villainy of the telephone, you raised your arms

like a child for a father and he lifted your dress, and in my mind
        it flitted for a second overhead then slumped in a corner—

an oversized, cloth balloon. After whatever actually happened,
        a charred smell saturated the air, blackened Chorizo in Pilsen.

In Chinatown furiously arguing love is more than the appropriate diodes
    snapped into position. After thrice denying I wanted you, then wanting

everything to do with you, the deer stampeded Ted and Doreen's
    glass overlook, and Ted hid in the bathroom till help arrived.

After I swore I would get out of Chicago, you threw your cell phone
    at my feet as if betrayed, as if I'd driven over a bridge

built with concrete and malice. After I left, I left
    my pens and plush tiger. After the world is over, I would like them back.

Love Song in the Style of Ramona

You render the landscapes of the dead long enough, and eventually
the guys come crawling. I used to love the way you would stack your victims
in photo albums. I used to love the simpering masses who loved you.
You squeezed my skeletal thigh. They have no decency, you said.
I want black cats to blanket us, I said. Even a breeze could have evicted us
from our bodies back then. Flashbacks to the blur of purple sand
at Big Sur clotted my dreams. I wanted to call you from the beach.
Then I did, a raisin speck against an eternity of sea cliffs.
Imagine flying a holding pattern over your own body
as you do in dreams of death. You looked so silly with that black-blue hair dye
spotting your pillow with violets. I used to dream of translating these flowers
into a language at some later juncture. Then your art electrified the undead
community with its sexual intensity—Abraham Lincoln begging to rip off
your blouse with its gold buttons, and with your feathers for eyes, you appeared
the clear goddess of timeless erotica. Of course you were Russian. Of course
the dead don't discuss such things, you said. No, I admitted,
the dead have no word for intimate and a thousand words for blind.

You Can't Spell Necromancy Without Romance

It isn't easy wandering the world eternally and scalping the progeny
of the proud, but there's a reason I picked you: I was bored.
It was Wednesday. Wherever you walked, people looked up.
Your stride reminded them of the awkwardness of a bull locked in a coatroom
and you'd have loosed yourself if only puberty had allowed. I felt for you:
the slave ship docked in your iris, the seeds of anarchism you spit
like spent matches on the ground. I imagined your turtleneck
and tights box stepping around the room, your glasses flying
in tight formation above. It's unclear what the objective of the exercise was
but it did remind me of some issues of delegation:
I need you to go back to 1975 and eat an hors d'œuvre. I need you
to tame a wild Taurus and teach Old Man Wilson a lesson
about the white-hot light that is love. It's a need-to-know
sort of operation, you know? I look into your eyes and no longer wonder
what makes any of us. Seventy-five impulses, eighty desperate demands,
an old Guatemalan love song you heard coming home on eighth street.
And hummed the three bars you knew while you put away beets
and Peter's Baked Beans. Your stubborn heart—the cave you shrank inside.
Panning away till you were so blurry, it was impossible to tell the music's origin.
So small and blurry the apartment and inkblot sky could have been anything.
And then they were.

St. Reuben Who's Never Been Kissed

St. Reuben is the patron saint of being thirteen and having an embarrassing
erection at the chalkboard. He is also the patron saint of skirt-lifting and didn't
make it long as a Disney Channel caricature. It's not funny. It's hilarious how life
on T.V. is more mellifluous than the way anyone lived it. The pink sun nursed
over the horizon at six in the morning, ascending into painful love.
Nothing you could even exaggerate into magic.
The amp yawning into the "on" position, the body-snatchers doing their thing.
The repeated requests for your body in particular went unanswered.
The auditorium bleachers became a tomb and, in lieu of graduation,
folded forward like a Labrador's tongue. And while St. Reuben
continued to claw his way down the Nielsen's after an episode
where he was caught reading "Busty Asian Beauties," you said I acquired a knack
for attracting girls in thick mirror glasses. You said, there are more forms
of vanity than you know and nothing like magic. I said, I'm tired of the machines
who exist only to instruct us about our lives and hold our hands while we're ill.
I worry that these kisses might never amount to a soul. About you
who lifted eyes like a saint, taking up your life like a holy relic
leaving it behind.

I'm Concerned You Will be Reincarnated as Office Supplies

If you do enough evil, maybe you come back as a tennis racket or a rhubarb pie.
If you do enough mediocrity, you come back as Rory the HP Office Deskjet.
And that will be the end of kite flying and no more visits to Red Robin, Kylie.
Now is the hour to make some endearing and life-changing errors
like mislabeling salt as sugar or breaking your home exercise equipment
in an effort to outpace a gazelle's reported land speed. One night hammered
in your bungalow in the Rocks, your husband and I agreed we must crash through
this world like bats blind from an attic. Yowling and colliding with vases
until caught. A falafel fell to the floor coating the carpet in iridescent baubles,
and I almost lost my place in the book of virtuous avians. You and Dana
drained a bottle of ill-considered choices in the ladies' room. Maybe
you drank away memories of your lives as staplers. Maybe somewhere
a grandfather steps in as a syringe to save his son from a peanut allergy.
We hollow out without utility. It's true. Even if you have to do life
round two as a shaker of thumb tacks, maybe you will hold a preschooler's
Venus in its elliptical orbit on the board. You always loved that sound of that:
elliptical.

It is I, Randall Knoper, and This be My Song

It is I, Randall Knoper, inventor of the fire-retardant sleeping bag and sole agent
        of the apocalypse. I'm here today to talk to you about values:

all my life, I've owned vacuums named for presidents.
        My CIA file is the new American standard in banality.

Because at age fourteen, when I dreamt of hell,
        I realized each of us is the subject of our own great experiment,

is mere inches from honking at another in anger.
        I'm asking for your vote in this upcoming deception.

In the belly of the white leviathan we call our nation's capital
        I shall be your Starbuck. Because our land is nothing like hell

where the sky collides with the mountains
        and you would whimper to hunger for anything. But here in this jungle,

I must ask you to surrender your vote to me, Randall Knoper,
        who defeated Eric the Red in a race across America.

Who, from the age of eight, has relished only the fantasy of going toe-to-toe
        with you, Lady Liberty. You would not love me for ingenuity

or ignominy but I will not die unnamed.
        I'm like a baby king crawling beneath a bawling moon.

Don't Die Alone in a Nuclear Holocaust, Bitter Flower

The most embarrassing position to die in during a nuclear holocaust:
eating a bag of Bugles alone, long after everyone else has left the office.
Go home, musty skeleton. Leave the scattered staples and toner cartridges
to the husk of a cleaning crew incinerated in the entryway.
Ruan Center drapes its worries over a bar district named for felons.
I used to take women to these rooftops. My limbs grew staunch
without learning much, except there's little mystery about the ways things work.
What's incredible is that fermented yeast plus a measure of dopamine
overwhelmingly governs much of the rest of your life sometimes.
Or sometimes making the cover of a magazine meant to document shame
might not turn you up Mr. Let's-Do-It-On-A-Laundry-Machine. Correction:
the worst position to die in is in your single mom's basement in the closet
with Jenny Holden, seventh grade, who was too homely for me anyway.
The worst is wishing for anything other than what you had at the end
where my sister and I watch coral sky scoot to the edge of vision and pass.
And Muffin the cocker spaniel, and these single living cookbooks,
this minestrone soup, earth and heaven will pass away,
but these words will never pass away.

Try as I might, I can't escape Melbourne. But in the National Gallery
I lose myself in your thicket, Meindert. Virile limbs blot out secrets
with burnet tusks. The vastness of your idea swallows its inhabitants
the way a boot swallows a whole ankle then spits it up again.
Nine months earlier, Nina unbuckled her boots, slipped off tights
and emptied herself onto the bed beside me. In my apartment
we stared at woodcuts of the apocalypse the next day
and the one after that. I can't hike outside that moment, can't board a plane
for the present—which may lie just beyond your brushstrokes.
Your pond which swallows me, the suffering of the old masters
cascading the walls. It's cold under your blanket of flotsam and sky.
Smoke signals can be seen. I think it's impossible to remain alive
without idolizing beauty even a little. Even if there comes a day you can't
even detect the smell of gas on your own fingertips. Like in "Love Liza"
where a suicide note burns down a house and takes a life in shambles
along with it. Yours is the metaphorical darkness we must acknowledge
at some point. The darkness which pushes the sun and shuts the doors
to the museum, the darkness which has somewhere to get to and sails calmly on.

Portrait of Self Seen in Shattered Glass

So if today I am split into infinitesimal pieces. If tides peck at me
a little of me washes up in Singapore or Shanghai. A little of me
in Tibet. If a little of me wanders through a diagram of the carbon system
which is only an analogy for one theorist's unhappy marriage—
the after dinner argument state, heartbreak over obvious infidelity state—
and today our postulates suggest the best minds of my generation
may be forever eating moo goo gai pan out of disposable white boxes
and be perfectly content and the formula for non-material happiness
is so visible that I just live it out as a test subject for my generation.
If such a thing is to be believed—my generation. And I wash up
in the unconscious of a several million year old rock formation
and later stumble back to your couch starved for human contact—
if this is the most acute need since I was fourteen and first encountered
female nudity in Mike Mahoney's attic, I am so naive. If you say
I am the portrait of a boy dashed against rocks and drowned. If you understand
the sea as a place like that, like desertion, where we can appear
with little or no comprehension and we may be swept into the arms
of something catastrophically giant—an atoll, a nebula of stratus—
and I would shed my belongings like unlikely gifts when I came home to you.
If today a part of me comes home to you, salts the sidewalks
of the women's college you walk, and you crunch me
into further shards. I can see myself in the overturned wine bottle,
the fluttering robe like a dancer's hand searching for hips.

For My Fellow Captive on Her Birthday

Six months ago we counted blades of grass added to vision by illumination
of floodlights. Reader, there are stories absurd enough to be true.
How a flighty woman lured a dancer and me to backwater NSW—
an alternate universe with one working phone, a general store stocked
only with hard alcohol, snake skins, overpriced ice cream. The star-blazoned sky
which could barely differentiate between the dead and living.
And at five in the morning, we left under the downpour of white dwarfs
with our suitcases and vanished from among the dead via school bus.
In Sydney, the stoplights sounded like Pac Man and I understood how he felt
relentlessly cornered and pursued by ex-wives. I wondered aloud
if Pac Man ever experimented with ecstasy and why could he eat the dead
only after ingesting fruit? What about Mary sweeping angel feathers
out of the entryway a couple thousand years ago? And now she's only an image
of an image. We sat in Sydney Harbor and I asked, Do you think this happens
to others? Broke and eating lamb off a stick at age twenty-six. Below the dock
hundreds of whiskered fish surfaced. You breathed in the ghost
and gave it up again. A Coke can came up for air.

Poem for My Thirty-Seven Mistresses

Poor, dirty, and wretched, living in a city full of crumbling ceilings
is no way to spend your early twenties.
I'm prepared to test an ordinary existence. To grow basil or sage.
To cultivate hobbies into age, the way a sailor might carry
a compass even after it shatters. You arrived at this earlier.
Brewed sweet tea, baked biscuits while I shaved my head
in pursuit of black-haired dervishes. Lean, angular women fit for wit
and worship, not Sunday afternoon at the store, and so I spent it by myself
writing bizarre fanfiction where Pikachu suffers from pica and the whole crew
learns a valuable lesson about the dangers of ingesting paint chips.
I keep my soap in a bag, my books in boxes, hide in the bathroom
and run water just to blot out my thoughts. Skin stained
from washing, a halo of epidermal products above, and I conceived all I wanted
was Illinois. Like my cousins who marry young
separate old, and behind the high school, the wind blows
new women into town. But, Robert, I'm a fool
for the stars who go down. My pillow's a face
I don't remember. You're looking at the last Soviet superman
eating a bowl of granola.

Satan and I take bets on who will die first. I bet
I will. Satan bets his fastball can outstrip the speed of sound.
Of course, neither of us actually owns a softball. I'm impoverished.
He's ethereal. So we just sit on the curb and lose count
of chestnuts hurtling into the grassy abyss, the bodies plummeting
from the train trellis like an old man's teeth into soup. When I'm older,
we'll go somewhere besides the dry goods store on a Saturday night, I say.
But the deceiver pricks his ears as if receiving a signal from a Russian spy plane.
Who's to blame him? We've spent whole nights repeating this epithet
to ourselves. We've held each other's hair over porcelain mouths
until we felt cleansed. Satan no longer bothers to appear
as a woman in white with nasty black teddy or a horrific cloud raining
blood and rotten apple cores. His name badge says Howard Winsome
and he is an alcoholic. We take bets on who will reach the porch first.
My money's on me. His is on me too. I take off like a badger
ripping into its new home. Satan stands and watches.
He is of two conflicted minds: the one thing he will not suffer
is to lose.

Three

God Brings Before Us a Series of Delectable Cakes

When God came down, you never imagined it would be as a cloud of fireflies.
You never imagined the Sleepy Time Bar & Hotel or the slow hiss of a door
which resounded for hours through the ice machine. The sea muttering
its futile threats from the talus-glutted beaches. I watched us happen
for an hour after we left Saint Mary's. On television, God always appears
via prism-perfect light, while demons manifest through smoke.
But fat smog marshaled onto the mountain and swooped down,
filling our August and coating the weeds tethering the beach.
Everything smelled like cake. The cake moon, the frosted ironworks caking it up
on the horizon. Isn't a fondue basically a delicious volcano waiting to happen?
I asked. You said that when you die, you have so many things you want to ask.
But you've never been happier than when we sat drinking jugs of Carlos
outside the animal print lounge, and neither of us positing much of anything.
When you aren't around, I go and sit on the grass. I eat some cake, and I listen
to the Lord. You drive home with a set of trinkets to see what I will call them—
comforter, cormorant. Lemon chiffon. Neither of us asks if we are lonely.
We eat the cake, and the question is the cake. Then comes the rapturous chirping
and all the sidewalks glazed with rain.

Elegy for What Won't Boil Down

I attempt to remember being formless, void
and only end up with the image of an iceberg absconding into a cosmos of seas.

God forced air into your cigarette-scarred lungs, scolded music into your digits.
And evening passed and morning came marking the several billionth some day.

You met it on the porch with the withered sitar, sang "The Great Physician"—
Oranges, apples, lemons and pears. I will kill you if you don't share

though your shelves were lined with the addict's fare: condiments,
the nightly veined brown bag. Because of a war your father

ferried over from a decade before, buried in a chest. Because of anemia
and the Velvet Underground, Roxy Music, the Stones.

And God said, *I see now how this could be hard.* And lying hungover on the
ottoman, you swore, *Let there be a dense mist of hopelessness.* And there was.

Had a vision of your black poodle who ate half a bag of sod before they caught
her, your mother the doe. Meanwhile, on a darker note, a man in Colorado

who would be rewarded with depiction in cinema sawed off his arm the hard way.
Catullus, who Kara says was the first true rock star, released a new edition

of the manual of lust. You read it, didn't buy it, refused to buy
anything short of spiritual starvation. If you could hear yourself,

not now, but two years before when you sounded like a young Lou Reed.
Satellite of love lost in impregnable space and mesmerizing but mangled renditions

with God hovering over the face of the water. *Was this what you intended?*
you demanded of the reflecting pool who ironically hadn't given this any thought.

There was once a single fruit which bloomed into a thousand guilts. I can carry
a word like that for years and never bother to utter it. See, the body

is no machine but is built to break like one and according to most recent scholars
cannot return to nothing. Even after fallen rock, intense poison

is what won't reduce, what makes you sick. The remainder of wind left in wind,
the sea mumbling to itself.

Some Piece of You Stays in Me, and I'll Never Give it Back

The fir trees, hundreds of fir trees, fill up the windows of the car.
I spend the evening quoting Rimbaud to an empty room. I come to my house,
my house with its weeping paint, with bags like wings under each arm.

The moon stands stupidly in the sky and doesn't inform me of anything.
Its ribs show through its skin like a piñata. After all this is over
I won't forget its sorry chirping, the way it meddled in our gravity

and washed over our socks and shoes. The things it said
by insinuation that made us sick, the way it covered your hair
like an oil slick, the way it lusted after you in the locker room.

The way its hair fell, and then it was plummeting too. The way
we watched the river burn in June, the blaze gliding over everything
and you wanted to take back the ugly thing you said.

You wanted to take back the moon and set it straight in the pond. To dust off
the firs who couldn't breathe under all the pollen that season and unfold
the corners of my books which gathered like accusations in the entryway.

The tuxedo cat which rolled onto its back like an apology
and me under the sour-faced moon like a stoic, considering
which wound to lick, wishing there were more.

Honesty is a blind dog wandering the chicken coops. You let it in
because you have no wife, no children. Flirtations with the neighborhood women,
the coat of an old stationmaster, and the long, snowy acre of your art. You sell
clothes to women with names without grace or assonance—Michelle,
Campbell—women who know nothing of cinema. How in "The White Ribbon"
it's the viewer who perhaps knowingly tortures the baron's son.
You connect the dots with Schrödinger's thoughts on felines and the inadvertent
destruction of love. A tear that you cover, but you keep it to yourself
push her plaid skirt to her ankles. And you do wonder about the dog.
Teaching him tricks like interrogate-the-suspect and how-to-beat-a-polygraph
won't keep him forever. Every day his bark a little fuller, photoreceptors signaling
allowing greater light. Soon he may remember enough to know who it was
who put him here. You said this was what you wanted,
said Sarah. Now, without others, you've become tangled up
in yourself. You clean lobster pots alone with your dog, polish your gun.

For My Father, Regarding My Law School Acceptance

Good news, Dad: in Monroe, Louisiana, an editor is wadding up this poem.
He arches his arms like some sort of air mantis and shoots it at a plastic trash can.
He misses. Everyone in the office cheers. They cheer because maybe
I will finally accept my admission offer from Vanderbilt Law. The editor
says, Huddle up team. The editor says, I'm going to read a poem aloud.
My goat is sad. My goat is green, he begins. It's a ballad about a Romanian
man's conscripted son. One editor sits at his desk reading an essay debating
Rasputin's nigh-invincibility. It's obvious his feet want to clamor up the desk.
His sweater wants to devour his neck. The editor is daydreaming of Sydney
and waddles over to unwad the poem to prove a point about scholarly integrity.
Nothing is happening in this stupid poem, he thinks. His eyes
run over the words "sex-boots," and he begins to recall his trip to Texas in 1963,
the trip that made him the man he is today. He runs his hands over
what appears to be a guitar case. He mutters something into the graffiti-streaks
of the newspaper stand. It's a cool afternoon in October. In a month's time
the editor will appease his father by filling out law school applications. Then
even the dead will go sleepless in the streets of Dallas, and he will watch them
clear and soggy through the scope of the rifle.

In Italy, the wedding procession sets off from the summit. The procession moves as dogs move: a little obtrusive, a little uneasy. You nudging some granite round as they go. A long dust follows. This is the wedding at which we are all guests. And feel ourselves located in the second life of things: the church's dress of lilacs, the lilacs, the gown's yawning lace. For a moment able to inhabit another's happiness.

When you were a small girl, these habitations, one afternoon, seemed so visible you felt you could have climbed to them. A source in the sky too far to see. A cloud covered it. Your date arrived. From this you learned to measure anyone by the bounds that hold them. You, for example, limitlessly unattainable and unbroken as you were. Movies could move you, twilight laugh its silver laugh to the grass, but not a soul could reach the cage you'd built. The blonde clock would reset, and the detritus of these would waiver in orbit above you.

Meanwhile, somewhere, the wedding continues as anything continues: elsewhere, in the high official's house (where anything anyone ever wanted happens). Hands entwine. A father eats his wedding cake. The cake could be a single point or multiple points depending on the arrangement of guests. The bride's uneasy bliss, the age and make of the procession as it passes. To calculate the impetus and momentum of each. To wonder about will, and why our own errors remain more livable, and in the end, just to get the gin.

Though in your mind you're a small girl again. The boulder inside your body rolled away under its own power. You knew the cave you saw was no cave at all, so you sat in the field and sketched it. A waterwheel went by. No one was learning Latin. Out of the cave, undersized, cream-colored birds came. The wheel sifted your body up and over. Some invisible shepherd had come to tend you. You were powerless to refuse.

I'm astonished no one has ever suggested that your sight has simply
preceded you into your following life. This isn't intended cruelly.
Like Siddhartha, but much less zealously, I based my life on a gamble
that the buds that die simply weren't intended for this particular act.
Resplendent snow varnishes the window where I repeat to myself
the host of Greek verbs all indicating departure. I embark, vamoose.
It's said when the body gives in to the corpse, the spirit has left it.
After your sight left you, my mother bought you an electronic reader
in the hopes your spirit would stop rattling you awake.
Tonight I want to write about something quiet and a thousand miles
distant. I want to run my hand over night and not feel it rotting beneath
my fingers. A liver sick from liquor, an example of the martyr I still might be
passes on a street in Richmond. I can say little about him except
he clutches his books to his chest, crosses the road.
Tomorrow when I peer into the mirror with the paint stain
like a flying buffalo, I will have internalized this, moved memory
into post-production. The scene where you hurl a ceramic angel
at the floor in frustration then laugh. The scene where you spray
what turns out to be the cat with a high-pressure hose.
This isn't intended cruelly. If anything is left in our body when we die,
I'm certain it's only what's cruel, what the spirit unconscionably bears.

Epistle Written in the Shadow of a Metal-Mache Horse

The poems discolored my life also, Frank. Honest. And now
these friends, this scrap iron horse is all I have to show.
I'm proud, Frank. Tired, Frank. My father's house is a frame
whose functions I hear but can't accurately interpret.
Sarah dated a skinny goat by your same name then broke his heart—
banging a fifty-year-old plumber while he passed out
on a pile of coats. Sarah was beautiful in a way that's hard
to forget which was all I asked for for my birthday and got it,
buried myself in another woman in Maine. Then the poems
dissipated all that into an afternoon of dusks, and it was 2007.
I had tape on my fingers and glue in my hair. Mangled innards
of a shoe. Many hopeful impressions of you. Let's go back
to your image of a mesa and your unwritten novel of Sancho Panza's
exploration of the Mexican West. Why did you bring me here?
Sancho asks. To have a heart is to risk it. To forge ahead, to live alone.
To go up as fire you must be frightfully burdened
and more human than anything.

Love Poem with Phantasmal Baseball Legend

If the ghost of Harry Caray himself were to finally materialize, this morning
couldn't get any more satisfying. Him, with his immense foam bat.
Us, watching a game show where the contestants guess at a number
secreted away in a silver box. And our breakfasts met with casual declaration.
No one can stop this from meaning something, you say—
the Sunday trips uptown to the art gallery or doing shots out of half a cantaloupe,
reprimanding that cheeky phantom who lashes out at us with feathers in the night.
It feels mysterious, like someone tickling my ancestor with a bat wing.
Meaningful, the way light repeats its patterns on the futon, flailing
onto a handle of almond liquor. Harry watches with us for a while
then is up reciting an ad for Armour hot dogs and beating the air with his bat.
Your eyes run over the box, transfixed, tracing its outline. You mumble
the number to yourself, but the contestants don't hear. They're busy cataloging
everything money will buy, which is opposite of this morning. Which is a comet
hurtling through our air space, leaving nitrogen-rich residue, the sky
thick with strata.

Idolatry

Then when I learned "Lost" was going off the air, I put on sackcloth
and smattered myself in ashes. There's something honest about my love
for fixed, commercial objects. Your Hello Kitty waffle maker sears animate faces
into my breakfasts. I am comfortable consuming my icons now.
I adjust the blinds, change the destination of light which has no capability
to recall its incredible journey to beckon uselessly from the patio.
At the end of the journey, the sadness is even greater for the fiction's weaver.
The army recruiter in the mall eats with his elbows over his food. I watch him
with the mixed emotions of a zoogoer looking in on an endangered wolf.
I feel like the lone, new washing machine in the sleazy laundromat.
Like the plane which crashes and burns fatally, but for the unbelievably lucky
but badly wounded in whom I want to believe.
Eat your waffles, you say. But I don't want my waffles. I'm sick
of these high-pressure sales situations, brooding into the half-eaten faces of others.

Poem for the Pegasus Fallen from Grace

I think of nothing but escape until I burst into the larger cave of sleep
and dream of one-eyed desperados. All the dead poets stowed away stars
like bags of letters, and they live on in them now.
Sometimes I can see their gas giants through the globular mists
that hover over March, and it's good to have your mouth to slide inside.
I've put away a star for you every year since I was twelve and knew
the wind could not shake the heavenly bodies from the juniper. They would sit
in the tree and ham it up, while we forgot every detail. Then came suitors,
and other fires, and barely holding it together. The fries
looked like they wanted to pounce on a packet of ketchup, you said.
I was the guy with a fortune cookie on every finger and little luck to spare.
And who, at nineteen, isn't desperate to wake up tangled up
with a woman on the carpet, frozen from the air conditioner?
Each eyelash a dark radius inviting you to its source, the stars climbing
the lattice work. Though what I said about luck was a lie
like what Perseus said to the Pegasus at the fountain.
Come look in my hand, he said. The night air is crisp as cedar and imagine
if the city could see the crown of but one wing.

Awe and Hallelujah

In a sudden moment of panic, you remembered you'd left an oven on somewhere
but kissed me anyway. Light, but like you meant it. Like the kitchen
might have burnt down already, so why not make it worth my while?
kind of kiss. I walked home like Lorca on his best day, falling in all the leaf piles.
I kissed the earth and lawn ornaments. I kissed thistles and bits of bark
begging for their jobs back on the cushy redwoods up the road. I kissed
a tamale vendor and his wife, four of her cousins. *Your tamales explode into jazz*
I said. I had no idea what this meant. I was being asked to leave the strip mall.
Someone said, *That man needs help.* Someone said, *It was terrifying.*
Like watching a blimp crash over and over into a helpless stadium.
I was asked to accept that I had kissed, that I would kiss again.
I was given a handout. I was handed a doughnut.
But back to you who by now had battled the blaze to minor structural damage.
Back to your friend, the French Canadian, who offered to buy us salvia.
I wanted to kiss her too, but by now I was being more closely monitored.
I didn't want to overplay my hand. A team of specialists was on hand. It seems
I'd been at this longer than I'd remembered—
a thousand years at least. All my pets had died. They said, *We need you, don't go.*
They said, *All hail the great, kissing god.* But how much longer must I tongue
the moon across this sky just to watch it twist away, come crawling back?

To Gracefully Accept One's Station

I need to say goodbye now. I'm off to find the wolf den where I was born.
For months, I'd been gluing gray fur to my face, and when you left
I raised my muzzle to the moon. A hand like a mother's
stroked my sable back. I know now I'd become like a glove left at a party.
I couldn't fit in the cup of anyone's palm and so poured myself into hermeticism
the way Prometheus forgot all else in his hatred of the gods. All winter
I growled at my pupils. Growled at the animals in the zoo, the snow,
the married women who begged to feel my coarse fur against their cheeks.
Then, when you left me a second time, when anxiety over pig sickness
reached critical pitch, I practiced extinction. I watched video of the dead
deer along the interstate. I tried to match their graceless stillness.
It wasn't all that hard, honestly, and now I am more them than myself.
I need to say goodbye now. To dig a hole to the other side of the earth.
To dash through extreme heat and pressure, dash through that desert—
a dark, strange Russia where even the piano does not love the pianist.
I can envision it already, the frozen earth flying from my toes.

Poem Set in Black and White with a Line from Bruce Bond

You walk through the window of a lonely movie and the line you're to deliver is
To grow huge in the mind is a fundamentally human enterprise, to grow
intrepid and tireless. And then a flowerpot falls on your head. At the crew table
you're seducing a watermelon and the crew member cutting it. And seduction
always feels like falling through a waterfall, like sliding into the icy ocean
after bonfires and vodka in Long Beach. My grasp of abstract realism
will never be enough to love you, says your character in the subsequent scene.
You puzzle over how and why the character delivers this line
with an origami octopus taped to his head. You puzzle over the efficacy
of the hero's soliloquy which blames the spread of nuclear arms
on one of the producer's upstairs neighbors. But what Michael Bay wants,
Michael Bay gets. And no one has ever lauded entertainment
or America for its credibility, the producers remind you.
In Lebanon, a boy who's also your son walks through the lonely movie of his life.
He can't remember the line he's meant to deliver, but you do.
And you desperately want to whisper it from the audience.
You desperately want to sprint into the shot and hold him so close he can't breathe
before the giant octopus is lowered, spraying this whole scene with ink.

The Poem is Not the Anatomical Heart

For Dean Young

The poet wants to rejoin the poem
even after behaving terribly and can't.
You aren't welcome because you're something else now.
An estranged father, a white noise of two lovers
lost in Malibu. One nervous. One naively fearless.
One ill-equipped for the rapidly aggregating promises
made by two of the damned rowing in tandem in the dark.
At a certain point, it's beyond forgiveness
and I couldn't positively tell you why.
In Hebrew, the word for *near* and *inside* sound nearly identical
told to a crowd at a party which one is asked to leave
for having two beyond too many, for behaving terribly.
Then back down the same fire escape, same sidewalks,
same phone buzzing into oblivion.
Like sometimes all that clots the wound
is *Don't call here drunk and late.*
One blameless. One half-conscious.
The stars tripping themselves up in the dark.
I have a failing organ, you say. I want to be forgiven.
And though asking isn't receiving, the soul has six wings
and roars. The shoreline tonight so calculated and cool.
There is not a person left worth forgiving you.

Sympathy from the Devil

When you laugh at Satan, the Lord laughs also. But Satan does not laugh
when you laugh at your own apish posture in the mirror. He has an antelope
look in his eyes. He doesn't love the way you don't love the gaunt stalker
entering and exiting the community college, the snow-mustached sedan
with the conscious math of a man counting every step till April. I wish she'd died
for what she did to you, he whispers when we are uptown for brunch.
There's a moon so massive that if you saw it you'd die instantly, he says.
I'm not especially convinced, but it's not totally critical. When you deny
Satan, it's not like confetti falls or heralding trumpets sound. You go on
relishing your Cobb salad on the promenade. I've never wanted to be an alien
more than that moment, to waltz around on that iron and nickel orb. No one
would collect my mail, except Satan who would need to be blindfolded
to bring it by. You've been away from the world too long, he says.
I know a girl. But I'm lost on the moon already, where you can never
say the same thing twice. No one can look in the mirror or speak above a whisper.
Not even light can touch you.

The Ship of Fools Happens into Paradise

If prayers are swift, if prayers move much faster than the light of stars
may you be loved while you are young and emit energy
onto far distant planets. Two days from shore:
trouble getting out of bed. My intended letters to you tickle the back
of my throat, but the blind midshipman shoots down a lovebird
who turns out to be first mate. My heart's not in it. Abducted
by daydreams of Minnesota and a lover who prays long enough for a palm
pressing just above her hips until it appears. This could be what the captain
sees as he feels his way along the hold—his daughter lighting an illegal candle
in her dorm. She never said to come home, not in so many words.
The remains of the lovebird sink into the sea unrepentant.
When I am lost, as often I am, I think of Maria—
her enormous breasts beneath her sweater, her holy black hair
and the angel of motherhood hanging over her. Midsummer now
in the city of monks where you are. If prayers are swift, may the words
I write be softer than the bread I eat. Softer than rain, the queen of mudslides.
Softer than orange peels, and may April bleed its scent into each of your picnics.
My name is Kyle McCord, and I serve the one you call YHWH.
I am telling you this in the tongue we were all made to forget, but which returns
from time to time, as the house cat unspooling in the sunlight dreams of claws.

Acknowledgments

The Adroit Journal: "Poem for Rude Birds." "To Sarah Lost in a Latin American Love Triangle."

Another Chicago Magazine: "The Elegant Universe."

I I I 0: "Bitterly Do We Break the Heart of God."

Anti-: "Love Song in the Style of Ramona," "Don't Die in a Nuclear Holocaust, Bitter Flower."

Barn Owl Review: "One Day You Wake Up and Your Life is Over."

Bellevue Literary Review: "The Poem is Not the Anatomical Heart," "The Ship of Fools Happens into Paradise."

Better: "What's Left."

Cimarron Review: "Elegy for What Won't Boil Down."

Cold Mountain Review: "I'm Concerned You Will be Reincarnated as Office Supplies."

County Music: "St. Reuben Who's Never Been Kissed."

Diode: "Dolphins, The Scientists are Discussing Your Enormous Brains," "Poem for My Thirty-Seven Mistresses," "Epistle in the Shadow of a Metal-Mache Horse."

Drunken Boat: "To Gracefully Accept One's Station."

Forklift, OH: "Man Dreaming of Collie Dreaming of Home."

Guernica: "They Said You Were to Be a Conquistador."

Gulf Coast: "The Soft Machinery of the Dark."

ILK: "On Meindert's Nature Which Swallows All Relics," "Sympathy from the Devil."

InDigest: "I Write You This on a Train Named for an Endangered Bird."

Interrupture: "Poem in Black and White with a Line from Bruce Bond."

Konundrum Engine: "The Ferry Took Me to the Mountain Pass."

The Louisville Review: "Some Admontions to the Architect of Lust."

Lungfull!: "Poem for Lars von Trier from the Heart of Missouri."

Meridian: "Portrait of Satan in Southern Arkansas."

PANK: "Poem Without Manners," "Childhood with Hypnopompic Overture," "Welcome to Unemployment, Massachusetts."

Phantom Limb: "To Me at Twenty-Six, Impoverished in Sydney," "Poem for the Pegasus Fallen from Grace."

Phoebe: "Like the Fox Scheming for Eggs."

Poetry City, USA: "It is I, Randall Knopper, and This be My Song."

The Rattling Wall: "Lycanthropy and You," "Portrait of Self Seen in Shattered Glass."

Red Lightbulbs: "For My Father, Regarding My Law School Acceptance," "Awe and Hallelujah."

Salt Hill: "God Brings Before Us a Series of Delectable Cakes."

Sixth Finch: "Useful Speculation."

Toad: "You Can't Spell Necromancy Without Romance," "Ginny in the Dutch Master's Grove."

Third Coast: "On String Theory and Other Problems of the Heart."

Volt: "Drawing Water from the Mountain."

Whiskey Island: "Faithful Poem to the Unfaithful Stars."

"The Ferry Took You to the Mountain Pass" appeared as a broadside from the Kalamazoo Book Arts Center. The incredible artist behind the broadside is Lauren Scharfenberg.

I'd like to thank the Vermont Studio Center, Bethany Seminary, and the art museums of Australia for giving me the time and support to write this work. I'd also like to thank The Philip Levine Prize, The Green Rose Prize, and Carnegie Mellon University for recognizing this book.

I'd like to thank my friends and editors who helped guide me: the astonishing Ezekiel Black, Kara Candito (FB2), Corey Marks, David McCord, Susan Steinberg, Megan Turner, my publisher Gold Wake Press, run by the tireless and talented Jared Michael Wahlgren, and Wendy Xu who constantly shocks me with her intelligence, generosity, and incredible heart.

To my fellow poets and teachers, Bruce Bond, James Tate, Dara Wier, Peter Gizzi, James Haug, Anne Waldman, and Fanny Howe, thank you. Along with my brother in poetry Keith Montesano, Joe Hall, Kristina Marie Darling, Traci Brimhall, Stephen Danos, Jeff Hipsher, Adam Day, Nick Sturm, Matt Guenette, the past and present staff of the Younger American Poets Reading Series, Rebecca Hazelton Stafford, Brian Mihok, and Jeannie Hoag

Thank you to my friends Michael Vasto, Thom Mahler, my sister and brother, Melissa Burton, Maura Walsh for her infinite going away parties, Kelsey Blessman, Andrew Tatge, Max Vilwock, Michael Fazio, Justin Bigos, Aaron Reed, and Monica Rice. And to the multitude of people who put together readings, gave me a couch or a bed to sleep on, or came out and supported me on tour or in the years that have followed, thank you for helping me do what I love.

Kyle McCord is the author of two other books of poetry: *Galley of the Beloved in Torment* (Dream Horse Press 2009) winner of 2008 Orphic Prize and a co-written book of epistolary poems entitled *Informal Invitations to a Traveler* (Gold Wake Press 2011). He's the 2012 recipient of the Baltic Writing Residency. Along with Wendy Xu, he is a co-founder of the Younger American Poets Reading Series and co-edits *iO: A Journal of New American Poetry*. He is a teaching fellow in the PhD program in Creative Writing at the University of North Texas in Denton, TX.

About the Cover Artist

Robyn O'Neil was born in Omaha, Nebraska in 1977, and currently lives in Los Angeles, California. Her work was included in the prestigious 2004 Whitney Biennial. She is the recipient of numerous grants and awards, including a Joan Mitchell Foundation Grant. She also received a grant from the Irish Film Board for a film written and art directed by her entitled "WE, THE MASSES" which was conceived of at Werner Herzog's Rogue Film School. http://robynoneil.com

CPSIA information can be obtained at www.ICGtesting.com
Printed in the USA
BVOW08s1018210114

342560BV00004B/172/P

9 780983 700173